x4/04

GREAT EXPLORATIONS

HERNANDO CORTÉS

fortune favored the Bold

PATRICIA CALVERT

BENCHMARK BOOKS

MARSHALL CAVENDISH
NEW YORK

For Jacob George Halbert
and Mickey Owen Elias—always with affection

With special thanks to Stephen Pitti, Yale University,
for his careful reading of this manuscript.

Benchmark Books
Marshall Cavendish Corporation
99 White Plains Road
Tarrytown, New York 10591-9001
Website: www.marshallcavendish.com

Library of Congress Cataloging-in-Publication Data

Calvert, Patricia.
Hernando Cortés: Fortune Favored the Bold / by Patricia Calvert.
p.cm. – (Great Explorations)
Summary: Describes the life of Hernando Cortés, the Spanish explorer who discovered Baja California and
explored the Pacific Coast of Mexico, but who is best remembered for conquering the Aztec Empire.
Includes bibliographical references and index.
ISBN 0-7614-1482-7
1. Cortés, Hernando, 1485-1547—Juvenile literature. 2. Mexico—History—Conquest, 1519-1540—Juvenile
literature. 3. Mexico—Discovery and exploration—Spanish—Juvenile literature. 4. Conquerors—Mexico—
Biography—Juvenile literature. 5. Explorers—Mexico—Biography—Juvenile literature. 6. Explorers—Spain—
Biography—Juvenile literature. [1. Cortés , Hernando, 1485-1547. 2. Explorers. 3. Mexico—History—Conquest,
1519-140.] I. Title. II. Series.

F1230.C835 C348 2002
972'.02'092—dc21

2002018462

Photo Research by Candlepants Incorporated

Printed in Hong Kong

1   3   5   6   4   2

Cover Photo and Inset: Art Archive/Army Museum, Madrid, Dagli Orti
The photographs in this book are used by permission and through the courtesy of; *Art Archive*:
Museo Ciudad Mexico / Dagli Orti (A),5, 9, 46; Science Academy Lisbon / Dagli Orti, 6, 15; National Palace Mexico
City / Dagli Orti, 12, 44, 58; Mirelle Vautier, 17, 23; National Palace Mexico City, 19; American Museum
Madrid/Album/Joseph martin: 24; Private Collection, Eileen tweedy, 27, 62; National history Museum Mexico
City/Dagli Orti, 29; Biblioteca Nacional Madrid/Dagli Orti, 31; Museo de America Madrid/Dagli Orti, 33; Galleria
degli Uffizi , Florence/Dagli Orti, 34; National Anthropological Museum Mexico, 36; National Archives
Mexico/Mireille Vautier, 42; Art Archive, 53, 65; Antochiw Collection Mexico/Mireille Vautier, 53; Biblioteca
Nazionale Marciana Venice/Dagli Orti (A), 67; Dagli Orti, 68. *Bridgeman Art Library*: Museo de America, Madrid
Spain, 28; Private Collection, 36. *Corbis*: 32, 55. *Art Resource/Scala*:\ 47.

Contents

foreword   4

ONE   The Quest for Gold   8

TWO   Cortés Seizes Control   14

THREE   The Christian Conqueror   22

FOUR   Fortune Always Favors the Bold   30

FIVE   Meeting Montezuma   41

SIX   Slaves to Greed   50

SEVEN   The Siege of Tenochtitlán   57

EIGHT   Everything Became Thorns   64

Afterword   73

Cortés and His Times   75

Bibliography   76

Further Research   77

Source Notes   78

Index   80

foreword

Anthropologists believe that nomads from Asia, traveling across a now-vanished land bridge spanning the Bering Sea, arrived in North America about 15,000 years ago. By 1250 A.D., a tribe from the north, which took its name from a mythical homeland called Aztlan, entered the Valley of Mexico. They called themselves the Aztecs.

They lived in caves and wore animal skins. Other tribes who had already settled in the valley scorned them as "the people of the dogs." No matter where the Aztecs stopped, they were driven away by more powerful neighbors.

At last they took refuge near the marshes and lakes of highland Mexico. Huitzilopochtli, one of the Aztecs' gods, had told them they would recognize their true home when they saw an eagle perched atop a cactus. In 1325, they saw such an eagle on an island in Lake Texcoco.

To make more space for crops, the Aztecs wove mats of reeds and mud called CHINAMPAS. These mats floated on the surface of Lake Texcoco. Cortés and his men were astonished at the beauty of the water gardens that drifted past as they entered Tenochtitlán in 1520.

They claimed the place as their own, built it into a great empire, and soon dominated the tribes that had despised them.

This rich civilization—with a population of more than three million, including Tenochtitlán, the third-largest city in the world—was completely unknown to Europeans, to whom the "real world" of trade and commence meant China and India. Christopher Columbus believed that by sailing west from Europe, a shorter route to the Orient could be found. He tried to convince wealthy patrons in his native Genoa, Italy, to finance such a venture. He appealed to King John II of Portu-

---

Christopher Columbus's critics believed he was foolish to sail west in an attempt to find a route to India. When Columbus landed on the Caribbean shores of Guanahani Island on October 12, 1492, he believed he'd achieved his goal.

Columbus primus inuentor Indiæ Occidentalis. VI.

gal and King Henry VII of England, without success. For six years, he pleaded with Queen Isabella of Spain to provide money for ships and men. In 1492, she finally agreed.

Columbus set sail with three small vessels, and landed on the shore of Guanahani Island in the Bahamas on October 12, 1492. He believed he'd reached the Indies, and called the natives "Indians". When he heard that a nearby island—Cuba—was rich in gold, he sailed there, too.

The discovery of unknown lands far to the west ignited fires of greed and ambition among the nations of Europe. In 1497, the Italian navigator Amerigo Vespucci followed Columbus's path across the Atlantic. He crossed the ocean three more times and described visiting a *mundus novus*, or new world. In 1513, Ponce de Léon sailed from Puerto Rico in search of the "Fountain of Youth," and found Florida instead. In 1519, Ferdinand Magellan began a voyage around the world and became the first European to set foot in what is now the Philippines.

Such discoveries, following swiftly one upon the other, inspired fierce competition among Europeans. In this environment, a Spanish boy named Hernando Cortés came of age. In no heart did the passion for gold and glory burn more brightly than in his.

O N E

The Quest
for Gold

When Columbus arrived in the New World, seven-year-old Hernando Cortés was playing boyhood games in Medellín, Spain. The village was located in the province of Estremadura, near Spain's border with Portugal. The rocky countryside, best suited for grazing sheep and goats, was nonetheless known for producing "famous races of men."

Cortés, an only child, was born in 1485 (the month and day aren't documented). The thick stone walls of the home Hernando grew up in kept it cool during hot Spanish summers. There was a *bodega* (wine cellar) in the courtyard, and the family's coat of arms was proudly displayed above the main entrance.

As a child, Hernando was frequently "so ill that he was often on the verge of death." His deeply religious parents discussed which of the Twelve Apostles should be named as their son's protector. Saint Peter

As a youth, Cortés had been thin; by the time of his arrival in Mexico, he was sometimes called Stout Cortés by those who knew him. He wasn't considered handsome in the ordinary sense, but his pale complexion and expressive eyes gave him a compelling demeanor.

POOR BUT PROUD

Hernando's parents, Martin Cortés de Monroy and Catalina Pizarro Altamirano, were *hidalgos*, which meant they came from noble but untitled Spanish families. As was true for many *hidalgos*, a noble name didn't guarantee wealth. Martin Cortés had retired from Queen Isabella's army and scraped by on a small pension. Hernando's mother's family had ties to a famous explorer—Francisco Pizarro, the conqueror of Peru—who'd also been born in Estremadura.

was chosen, and to the end of his days Hernando gave Saint Peter credit for helping him endure the hardships life had in store for him.

As time passed, the boy's health improved. He played war games with his friends at the foot of Medellín Castle, situated on a treeless knoll near the village. Hernando became an expert horsemen and hunted rabbits with his father's greyhounds. He was so active that his father called him a "rushing river."

In 1499, at age fourteen, Hernando was sent to the University of Salamanca, one hundred miles northwest of Madrid. His parents wanted their son to prepare for a career in law, a profession that might bring him wealth and honor.

In Salamanca, Hernando lived with his aunt, Ines de Paz, studied Latin grammar, and acquired many friends. Those who knew him at the time described him as a slender but muscular young man, about five feet four inches in height. His skin was unusually pale, making his dark eyes seem especially bright.

Cortés became discontented with the future that had been chosen for him, partly because his fellow students came from rich families, while money was always a problem for the less affluent Cortéses. After two years at the university, Hernando gave up his studies. His parents had expected great things of their son, and were greatly disappointed when he returned home.

Young Hernando might have fit the description of a modern teenager, for he "made much noise in the house of his parents . . . he was turbulent, haughty [and] restless." In spite of the family's modest means, Cortés indulged himself by gambling. He apparently played for the love of the game, because friends said he showed "as good a face to losses as to gains."

Hernando craved a life of action and, because he came from an impoverished family, he was tantalized by tales of gold and treasure in the New World. On September 3, 1501, Nicolas de Ovando, a distant relative, was appointed by Queen Isabella as a governor-general in the West Indies. Driven to distraction by their son's conduct, Hernando's parents didn't object when he announced his intention to go to the Indies with Ovando.

Before he could leave, however, Hernando—now seventeen—was involved in a romantic escapade that nearly killed him. As he left the second-story window of a ladylove, he leaped down onto a stone wall, which collapsed beneath him. He was buried under a pile of rubble, and his back was severely injured. On February 13, 1503, Ovando sailed for the Indies as planned—but Hernando lay in bed, recuperating from his misadventure.

For more than a year, Hernando wandered about Spain. Then, in 1504, he paid twelve ducats for passage on the *Trinidad*. The ship's des-

SLAVERY IN THE NEW WORLD

Spanish colonization of the New World depended on the invaders' ability to exploit the natural wealth of the area. However, the Spaniards had belonged to an elite class in their homeland, and were too proud to do common labor. Yet the fields of corn, cotton, sugarcane, and cocoa needed to be tilled and tended. The natives of islands like Hispaniola, who possessed no modern weapons and could offer no adequate resistance, were an obvious source of what the Spaniards needed most: men and women who could work the fields. Therefore, one of the first steps the Spaniards took upon their arrival in the New World was to subdue the native people and force them into slavery. Uprisings were common, and often the natives simply vanished into the jungle.

The Spaniards who came to the New World believed common labor was beneath them. Consequently, the native population were forced into slavery. Those who tried to escape were severely punished.

tination was Santo Domingo, the Spanish colony on the West Indian island of Hispaniola where Hernando's kinsman, Ovando, was headquartered.

The *Trinidad*'s master, Alonso Quintero, was a trader whose vessel was one of four bound for the colonies with supplies. Quintero was anxious to be the first to arrive, so that he could sell his merchandise for the best prices. When the ships stopped to take on fresh water in the Canary Islands, Quintero sneaked off in the middle of the night to get a head start. His plan backfired. A storm came up, snapping the mast of his ship and forcing it back to port. He was the last to dock in Santo Domingo, long after his competitors had sold their goods.

Upon arriving on the island, Hernando discovered that Governor Ovando was away. However, he was advised by another official to apply for a grant of land, settle down, and establish a plantation. That wasn't what the young adventurer had in mind. Columbus had returned to Spain with tales of gold, and Hernando was impatient to gain such riches for himself.

Nevertheless, he heeded the suggestion. He took up farming near the village of Azua and became the owner of several Indian slaves. His primary crops were sugarcane, cotton, corn, and cocoa. He later became one of the first Spaniards to import cattle to the Indies. Within six years, he had accumulated a comfortable fortune.

Success as a plantation owner didn't dim Cortés's plans for adventure. Becoming a farmer had but one purpose: to acquire wealth, which in turn would allow him to engage ships, hire soldiers, arm them, then pursue the explorer's path. As he'd remarked on his arrival in Santo Domingo, "Neither in this Island nor in any other of this New World, do I wish . . . to stay long. I came to get gold, not to till the ground like a peasant."

T W O

Cortés Seizes Control

In 1509, Cortés went on a mission to the western part of Hispaniola, where months before the Spanish had killed some rebellious Indians. Whenever slaves escaped, Cortés could be counted on to lead an expedition into the jungle to bring them back. Yet a gentleman farmer's life grew duller each day. Hernando told friends he'd prefer to "dine to the sound of trumpets or die on the scaffold."

Because of his zeal, Hernando caught the attention of Diégo Velasquez, captain of the military forces in Hispaniola. In 1511, Governor Ovando assigned Velasquez the task of bringing Cuba, the largest of the West Indian islands, under Spanish control. Velasquez—who was pink, portly, and forty-six years old—knew he needed someone more capable than himself to subdue the Cuban natives, and invited the twenty-six-year-old Cortés to accompany him.

Cortés gladly accepted, and in the process of bringing Cuba under

As far as the Spanish were concerned, the New World meant "New Spain." In this 1563 map, mapmakers depicted Florida, Cuba, Hispaniola, and Jamaica in an illustrated atlas.

Spanish control made himself even more popular with Velasquez. Because the venture was successful, Velasquez was given a governorship and established his headquarters at Santiago. In turn, he rewarded his lieutenant with new land grants and more slaves.

Years before, a foiled romance in Medellín had kept Cortés from sailing from Ovando. Once again, an affair of the heart complicated his life. A man named Suarez had brought his four sisters to Cuba, hoping to marry them off to wealthy Spaniards. Cortés courted Catalina, the oldest, promised to marry her, then lost interest in becoming a husband.

Suarez complained to Velasquez, who in turn ordered Cortés to live up to his pledge. Cortés declined. *No* wasn't a word that Velasquez liked to hear. He ordered Cortés thrown into prison. However, keeping him there was another matter. Hernando escaped and took refuge in church, where he knew Velasquez wouldn't dare pursue him.

A few nights later, when Cortés sneaked out to visit friends, he was seized by Velasquez's men, escorted to a ship bound for Spain, and offered a choice—marry Catalina or go home. Cortés wasn't a fool. He married Catalina, built her a fine house, and settled down. Velasquez was satisfied, and appointed Hernando the *alcalde*, or mayor, of Santiago.

On February 8, 1517, Francisco de Cordova, a fellow Santiagan, set out to explore the new lands between Cuba and Honduras. He was blown off course and, three weeks after leaving port, ended up on the Yucatán Peninsula, about 120 miles away from Cuba. Until then, its existence hadn't been known.

Cordova observed that the Indians who met him were haughty, rather than humble, as were the island natives. They were beautifully dressed in finely woven cotton garments fastened with gold clasps. Their houses were built of whitewashed stone, not thatch and wattle. The natives weren't merely haughty, they were hostile, and in the battle that ensued, fifty Spaniards were killed, two were captured, and

THE SPANISH DISEASE

It was said that Spaniards suffered from "a disease that could only be cured by gold." The malady—which infected all Europeans—was greed. The Indians' descriptions of the Spaniards' behavior was unflattering indeed. "They stuffed themselves with it, and starved and lusted for it like pigs," the Indians later told Father Bernardino de Sahagun. "They were slaves to greed."

Most Spanish adventurers, including Cortés and his men, were interested not in exploring new lands, but in acquiring riches. Finding gold in the New World and the prospect of instant wealth was much more appealing than other professions, like farming. When it was donated to the Church, gold was thought also to ease a man's passage into heaven. Gold, it seemed, bought comforts not only on earth, but in heaven, too. As a result, the *conquistadores*, or conquerors, were prepared to do whatever was needed to get it.

A solid gold breastplate depicts the Mixtec Indians' god of death. Aztec art was strongly influenced by this earlier culture. The Spanish ignored the god's grisly smile of such a god; only the gold mattered.

Cordova himself was wounded. He died two weeks after returning to Cuba, but not before telling Velasquez what he'd seen.

In May 1518, Velasquez outfitted four ships for a second expedition. He put his nephew, Juan de Grijalva, in command of 250 men and sent them back to the mainland. Grijalva traded the cheap trifles he'd carried with him (the green glass beads seemed to please the Indians) for several gold plates and elegant pieces of jewelry. Before they ventured farther up the coast, he sent one of his captains, Pedro de Alvarado, back to Cuba with the treasure.

Velasquez was astonished at what Alvarado set before him. Like Cortés, he dreamed of riches, and was annoyed that Grijalva hadn't immediately subdued the Indians and established a colony under the Spanish flag. Who could he chose for a more ambitious expedition? Velasquez hesitated. He didn't want to send anyone who might be as greedy as he was himself.

It was suggested that Cortés, who had accumulated a small fortune and had an appetite for adventure, would be just the man. "I knew him to be . . . full of courage," Velasquez agreed. "I have great confidence in him." Cortés was appointed the *caudillo*, or leader, of a third expedition. It was a choice that Velasquez regretted for the rest of his life.

Of course, treasure wasn't the only thing on Velasquez's mind. He reminded Cortés, "above all things . . . the Spanish monarch had most at heart . . . the conversion of the Indians." Hernando, a devout Catholic, hardly needed such advice.

Cortés, now thirty-three years old, no longer resembled the frail boy from Medellín who'd often been close to death. He was thick through the torso, his legs bowed from his having spent so much time on horseback. His face was too narrow to be called handsome, his beard too thin to be attractive, yet his large dark eyes were as compelling as ever.

Cortés believed that he conquered New Spain not only for gold, but also for the Christian God. After the Aztecs were defeated, he asked King Charles I to send additional priests, so that the Indians could be baptized. This painting is from a mural by the Mexican painter Diego Rivera, 1886–1957.

A gambler at heart, Hernando welcomed the chance to take charge of such an expedition. He recruited other *hidalgos* in Cuba to join him. He invested his own fortune in the venture, borrowed from friends, and mortgaged his plantation to get money to equip ships and to buy arms and food for his soldiers.

A SHARE OF THE PROFITS

In Cortés's day, kings and queens paid part, but not all, of the expense of a foreign expedition. It was necessary for explorers to assume some of the cost themselves. Often, they had to equip their own ships, recruit soldiers, then provide them with food, clothing, and arms. The advantage of such a shared arrangement was that an expedition's leaders were allowed to keep part of the profits for themselves. The disadvantage was that too often, they ravaged the lands they came upon, stuffed their pockets, and considered the consequences of their behavior later, if at all.

Hernando knew that the Indians were afraid of horses, which had never been seen in the New World until the Spanish arrived. He took sixteen cavalry mounts with him, the better to intimidate the natives along the Yucatán coast. His own horse, a hot-tempered chestnut named Arriero, was certain to make a deep impression.

Before Cortés left Cuba, however, Velasquez was told by Cortés's enemies that Hernando intended to keep whatever riches he found for himself. Velasquez hastily revoked the commission he'd given Hernando, and put Vasco Porcallo in charge of the fleet instead.

Cortés Seizes Control

When whispers reached his ears that he'd been deposed as *caudillo*, Cortés reached swiftly. He gathered ten ships, 350 soldiers and 100 marines, ten cannons, and four smaller pieces of field artillery (brass cannons called falconets). At dawn on November 18, 1518, before Porcallo could take command, he sailed from Santiago.

Among those on board was Pedro Alvarado, who had made the voyage with Grijalva. One of the youngest *hidalgos* was twenty-two-year-old Gonzalo de Sandoval, whom Cortés fondly called *hijo*, or son. Also present were Father Olmedo, a Dominican monk, and Bernal Diaz, who later recorded the details of the expedition.

Velasquez "roared with rage" when he discovered what Cortés had done. When Hernando took on fresh water and supplies in Havana, at that time located near the western end of Cuba, Velasquez sent word to the port commander to arrest him. The sight of so many well-armed men accompanying Cortés kept the port commander's tongue silent.

As the fleet prepared to head for the Yucatán, Cortés called his men together. "Years from now," he said, ". . . men will point to you and say to their children, 'There is a hero, he was with Cortés in New Spain.'" Yet he hadn't forgotten Velasquez's reminder to convert the natives to Christianity.

"We seek not only to subdue boundless territories in the name of our Emperor," he added, "but to win millions of unsalvaged souls to the True Faith. . . . Be true to me, as I am to you, and I will load you with wealth such as you have never dreamed of. This wealth will not be won easily—but who is afraid?"

Hernando Cortés was not. Without a backward glance, he left behind a wife, a fine home, and a plantation. The call of glory, gold, and God was one he couldn't refuse.

THREE

The Christian Conqueror

No sooner had Cortés's fleet left Cuba than it was caught in a storm. One of the vessels was badly damaged and had to be escorted to Cozumel, an island off the coast of the Yucatán Peninsula, for repairs.

Cortés's ship was the last to drop anchor, and when he went ashore he was infuriated to discover that Alvarado had plundered a *teocalli*, an Indian prayer house, and stolen food from the natives. How could Indians' hearts be won for Christ if they were treated badly? Cortés demanded. Alvarado, a high-spirited fellow who also came from Estremadura, was ordered to return the stolen items.

While waiting for the damaged ship to be repaired, Cortés sent three vessels to the mainland to seek information about white men who were said to have been captured by the Indians during Cordova's expedition. Then he set out to explore Cozumel. He discovered the well-built limestone houses that Cordova had spoken of, and a cross that he

THREE GREAT EMPIRES—
MAYA, INCA, AND AZTEC

It's easy to confuse the three great empires of the southern hemisphere, which existed at different times and in different places. The oldest was that of the Maya, on the Yucatán Peninsula, which had fallen into decline by the 1400s. The Inca rose in the fifteenth century in the Peruvian Andes and included the citadel of Machu Picchu. The Aztec empire in the heart of Mexico, the youngest and richest of the three, was less than two hundred years old when Cortés discovered it in 1519.

When Cortés and his men landed at Vera Cruz in 1519, they were treated cordially by the Indians, who remembered the earlier expedition of Juan de Grijalva. The Indians gave Cortés gifts of beans, meat, fish, and corn cakes. In return, Cortés presented the Indians with beads, pins, needles, and scissors.

believed was proof of previous Christian influences. (He was mistaken. It was a Mayan symbol for the god of rain.)

Cortés discovered something else that deeply disturbed him. The bloodstained altars of the temples indicated that the Indians practiced

Cortés, who showed no mercy in battle, was sickened by the ritual sacrifice of human beings as practiced by the Aztecs. He told Montezuma the evil custom must be abandoned immediately, but Montezuma refused.

---

human sacrifice. He toppled the statue of one of their heathen gods and put a wooden image of the Virgin Mary in its place. He lectured the Indians about their evil practice, and ordered that the temple be cleaned and whitewashed.

Two weeks later, the ships returned from the mainland without news of captive white men, but soon afterward a large canoe approached Cozumel. In it were several Indians, among them a man whose hair was shorn like a slave's. He called out in Spanish, "Gentleman, are you Christians?"

Thirty-year-old Geronimo de Aguilar, a Catholic priest, had been shipwrecked eight years earlier and become the slave of a *cacique*, or Indian chief. Aguilar had managed to earn his freedom from the chief who had captured him, and Cortés welcomed him with a warm embrace. He was glad to rescue a fellow Spaniard, but more importantly, he knew Aguilar would be valuable as an interpreter.

On March 4, 1519, Cortés's fleet sailed around Cape Catoche on the Yucatán Peninsula and proceeded west and then south to the Grijalva River, where the Tabascans lived. The river was too shallow to navigate, and the ships had to anchor offshore. Cortés had the men take small boats to the marshy shore. As the Spanish entered the river, they saw along the banks and among the mangroves thousands of natives armed with spears and bows and arrows, ready for battle. The Indians yelled and blew horns and forbade the Spanish to land. Cortés managed to find a safe beach for his men to spend the night.

The next morning, some Indians came to the camp and offered the Spaniards food. But Cortés wanted more than food—he wanted permission to enter their town. The Indians refused, and in the battle that followed, the Spanish took the town, eighteen Indians were killed, and Cortés lost his shoe in the muddy ground.

Cortés learned three important things in his first face-off with the natives of Mexico. First, Spanish artillery was critically important. Second, although the Indians outnumbered the Spanish ten to one, their primitive weapons inflicted little damage. Finally, the Indians' armor (thick, quilted cotton vests) was useless against Spanish swords and gunfire.

The next day, the Indians again brought food, and this time they also brought gold to the Spanish. But the Spanish once more were dissatisfied. They headed into the Indians' fields near the town of Cintla, and fighting broke out.

The bloody battle spilled over to the next day, March 25. The marshy land, crossed by creeks and drainage ditches, made it difficult for the Spaniards to use their cannon and crossbows to maximum effect, but the cavalry was another matter. Cortés, accompanied by a dozen men on horseback, charged into the fray. Francisco de Morla, one of Cortés's boldest soldiers, clad in gleaming metal helmet and breastplate, and mounted on a snorting dapple gray, produced terror among the natives. Cortés later exclaimed, "These Indians . . . believe that [horses] go to war of their own accord!" The occasion marked the first time horses were used in battle in the Americas.

When the fight was over, one hundred Spaniards were wounded, but an estimated eight hundred Indians lay dead. The Indians asked permission to bury their dead, and after it was granted, they offered the Spaniards meat and corn cakes, gold and turquoise jewelry, and twenty female slaves.

Among the slaves was a nineteen-year-old girl the Indians called Malinche. Later, the Spaniards baptized her and christened her Marina. She spoke Nahuatl, the language of the highlands, as well as Mayan, the language of the lowlands. Aguilar spoke Mayan and Spanish. Thus, Marina was able to translate Nahuatl into Mayan, which Aguilar then translated Mayan into Spanish.

Cortés used the occasion to demonstrate before the Indians the power of Spanish artillery and horses. He had a cannon fired and a high-spirited stallion brought out, rearing and snorting before the astonished Indians.

Through his interpreters, Cortés asked the Indians where their gold and silver mines were located. They replied that they had none, and were not interested in the precious metals, but that it was quite different in the Valley of Mexico. There, a fabulous city called Tenochtitlán had been built on an island in a lake. Its streets were wide, and its inhabitants wore jewelry of gold, silver, jade, and other precious materials. Its citizens called themselves Aztecs, and were ruled by an emperor named Montezuma.

Cortés's conquest of Mexico began with a confrontation with Indians along the Tabasco River in March 1519. The Spaniards were stunned when hundreds of painted Tabascan warriors, armed for battle, sailed their dugouts out of mangrove swamps along the river's bank.

Gold . . . silver . . . jade. The words were the ones Cortés had been waiting to hear.

By Good Friday, April 21, 1519, Cortés fleet lay a mile off the mainland of Mexico. He went ashore with the men, cavalry, and artillery, and a few dogs. The dogs—European mastiffs weighing as much as 150 pounds (68 kilograms)—terrified the natives who had gathered on the beach. They owned only small, barkless dogs that were often used as food.

An Indian Princess

Marina's original Indian name was the same as the name of the twelfth month of the Mexican calendar. Her father was a lord, or *tlatoani*, of a village near Coatzaloalocos, but he died when she was a child. When she was eight years old, her mother sold her to wandering slave traders in order to give Marina's portion of her father's inheritance to her favored son. Because Marina could translate Nahuatl into Mayan, Cortés quickly realized that she would be invaluable as an interpreter. Marina soon became a trusted confidante, was baptized into the Catholic faith, and later gave birth to two of Cortés's sons. One historian estimated her importance to Cortés's expedition as "equivalent to ten bronze cannons."

After the Spaniards defeated the Tabascan Indians, Cortés was given twenty female slaves as a peace offering. A nineteen-year-old Indian princess named Marina was among them. She soon became one of Cortés most trusted advisors.

The route (in red) indicates Cortés's march inland, to Tenochtitlán, the Aztec capital. The arduous journey took two and a half months, and covered 250 miles through snow-covered mountain passes.

Cortés was greeted warmly, however, because the Indians remembered Grijalva and his gift of green glass beads. Cortés was presented with plates of copper and silver, then with food such as beans, corn cakes, fish, and roast turkey. In return, he gave the Indians more beads, as well as pins, needles, scissors, and small mirrors.

Then Cortés asked the Indians the question foremost in this mind—did their emperor, Montezuma, possess gold? *Yes* was the answer. It was a fateful reply, one that doomed not only Montezuma, but also his entire kingdom.

F O U R

Fortune Always Favors the Bold

News of the Spaniards' arrival was relayed to Montezuma, who was not completely surprised. Several years earlier, events had taken place in Tenochtitlán that predicted the return of an ancient Aztec god, Quetzalcoatl. In 1510, Lake Texcoco had overrun its banks, flooding the countryside. A year later, an Aztec temple had burst into flames for no reason. Then three comets had suddenly appeared in the sky.

Montezuma had summoned a *tonalpouque*, an astrologer, to interpret the signs. He was told they meant the empire would collapse when Quetzalcoatl retured.

Now Montezuma saw that strangers had gathered offshore in water houses (ships). They possessed frightening dragons (horses). Their weapons belched flame (cannons). Montezuma's "heart [was] anguished," and he wept to think the astrologer's prediction had come true.

In 1519, Montezuma saw a comet from the rooftop of his palace in Tenochtitlán. A TONALPOUQUE—an astrologer-priest—told the emperor it foretold the return of Quetzalcoatl, the plumed serpent god.

Nevertheless, the emperor decided to play for time. He sent emissaries to the coast, bearing presents for the strangers—chests filled with necklaces, earrings, and bells made of gold; small gold statues of ducks, lions, jaguars, deer, and monkeys; and elaborate feather headdresses in brilliant colors.

Cortés gladly accepted the gifts, but insisted on thanking Montezuma in person. The emissaries replied that their emperor wouldn't receive him, nor did his health permit him to come to the coast. Instead, even more fabulous gifts were offered. Food arrived, too, but to the

QUETZALCOATL RETURNED

Quetzalcoatl, the plumed serpent (*quetzal* was a bird of brilliant plumage; *coatl* was a fanged snake), was a part-man, part-god of Aztec myth. He was black-skinned and much loved by his people. According to legend, ". . . sorcerers attempted to shame him into making human offerings . . . [but] he would not consent." Enemies drove him into exile, but before Quetzalcoatl—also called the warrior of the dawn—sailed to the east in a boat made of snakeskins, he promised to return.

The head of the plumed serpent god Quetzalcoatl adorns a temple built in his honor in Teotihuacan, Mexico. According to legend, Quetzalcoatl was driven out of the Aztec empire because he opposed human sacrifice, but he promised to return.

Spaniards' horror it was sprinkled with blood from recent human sacrifices.

Shortly after Montezuma's emissaries departed, twenty Totonac Indians from several miles up the coast paid Cortés a visit. They had

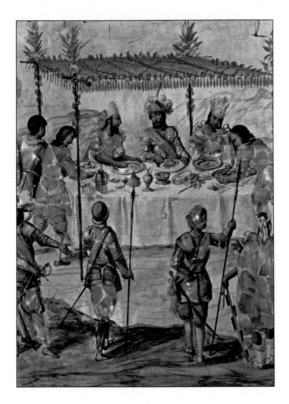

Cortés hosted a banquet for ambassadors sent to him by Montezuma. Later, Montezuma returned the favor by presenting food to the Spaniards, who were appalled to see that it had been sprinkled with fresh blood from human sacrifice.

been conquered by the Aztecs, and they resented paying taxes to their rulers. In addition, they were dismayed by the Aztecs' demand for Totonac boys to be sacrificed on the altars of Tenochtitlán.

Cortés inquired how many warriors the Totonacs had. One hundred thousand was the reply. By comparison, Cortés commanded a mere few hundred soldiers. He realized that thousands of Indian allies would greatly increase his bargaining power with Montezuma. He advised the Indians not to pay any more tribute to the *calpixque*, the Aztec tax collectors. The suggestion frightened the Totonacs, but when Cortés promised to protect them with his cannons and cavalry, they agreed to swear allegiance to him.

In June 1519, Cortés began building *la Villa Rica de la Vera Cruz*, "the Rich City of the True Cross," on the eastern edge of the Mexican coast. Fresh water and game were plentiful, and Cortés worked side

THE SPANISH KING WASN'T SPANISH

Charles I, the descendant of Queen Isabella and King Ferdinand, was born in Ghent in 1500. On his father's side, he was descended from the Hapsburg kings of Austria. In 1516, upon the death of his Spanish grandfather, the sixteen-year-old boy ascended to the Spanish throne as King Charles I of Spain, even though he'd been raised by his Austrian relatives. His native tongue was French; his second language was German; he never learned to speak Spanish. The Hapsburgs were devoutly Catholic, and when Charles also ascended to the Austrian throne, as Charles V in 1519, he dreamed of reclaiming the power of the Holy Roman Empire.

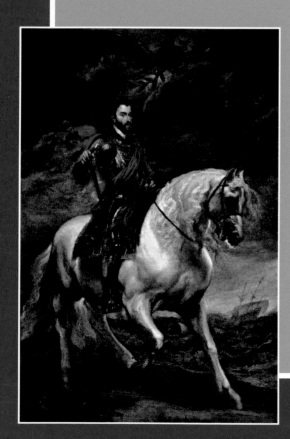

King Charles I of Spain.

34

by side with his men. Native craftsmen made sun-dried bricks for the project, and two months later a settlement arose that boasted a walled fort, church, storehouses, and barracks.

Cortés had shrewdly founded the new Spanish town entirely on his own, and declared himself to be its mayor. He then began dealing directly with the Spanish king, Charles I, by dutifully sending him a ship loaded with "the king's fifth" of the wealth he'd discovered. His action was the equivalent to cutting Velasquez completely out of the picture. Then, having established a permanent base, he was ready to head inland.

According to Spanish law, it was illegal for any Spaniard—no matter his title—to proceed with exploration without specific permission from the king. Cortés had never received such permission. He was a high-stakes gambler, however, and was determined to forge ahead, regardless of the fine points of the law. He also brushed aside the fact that he'd been told he wouldn't be welcome in Tenochtitlán. The lure of gold, silver, and gems was worth any risk. A Spanish proverb perfectly summed up Cortés's philosophy: "Fortune always favors the bold."

Yet the men who'd remained loyal to Velasquez believed Cortés had grossly exceeded his authority, and wanted the expedition to return to Cuba. Seven of them plotted a mutiny. The moment Cortés heard of it, the ringleaders were arrested. (Reacting swiftly to threats became his greatest strength.) Two of the plotters were sentenced to be hanged. The feet of one man were ordered cut off. Others were to be given two hundred lashes.

The sentences apparently weren't carried out, but Cortés succeeded in terrifying everyone else into submission. The truth was, he couldn't return to Cuba. His refusal to obey Velasquez's order to give up command of the fleet meant he was a traitor. In Cuba, he'd be put on trial and possibly hanged. Yet the attempted mutiny made Cortés realize that he must put an end to the division of loyalty among his men.

With the exception of one small vessel, the crafty Cortés stripped his ships of their sails, tackle, and hardware. Holes were drilled in the ships' sides, and then the ships were sunk in the harbor of Vera Cruz. He told his men that termites had made the vessels unseaworthy. Now there was only one leader to follow, Hernando Cortés, and the only path led inland, to confront Montezuma.

Some of Cortés's men talked of mutiny when he announced plans to go inland to confront Montezuma. Cortés countered the threat by scuttling his entire fleet in the bay at Vera Cruz. Without ships, the men had no choice but to follow him to the Aztec emperor's capital.

Cortés's Route, 1519 - 1535

Santa Fe

RIO GRANDE

MEXICO

Tenochtitlán
(Mexico City)

Veracruz

PACIFIC
OCEAN

MISSISSIPPI RIVER

St. Augustine

GULF OF MEXICO

CUBA

ATLANTIC
OCEAN

Aztec Empire

On August 16, 1519, with a force of four hundred to five hundred men, fifteen horses, and a few small cannons, Cortés proceeded toward the Mexican highlands. A small force commanded by Juan de Escalante remained behind to protect the settlement at Vera Cruz.

The coastal area had been hot and humid. By contrast, the climate of the high Mexican plateau was exhilarating. Days were clear; nights were cool. The first major village they entered was Jalapa, 4,000 feet (1,219 meters) above sea level, and in the distance the 18,700-foot (5,700-meter), snowcapped peak of Orizaba could be seen.

Along the way, Cortés was pleased to encounter tribes like the Totonacs, who also resented paying taxes to the Aztecs. As before, he encouraged them to stop paying the *calpixque* and promised to free them of the demands of their oppressors.

In every *teocalli* the Spaniards came upon, there was further evidence of human sacrifice. When the expedition got closer to Tenochtitlán, a temple filled with fifty bodies was discovered. The Spaniards themselves were not known for showing mercy to their enemies, but they were sickened by the pagan murders of the Aztecs.

The Spaniard's relatively peaceful progress toward Tenochtitlán ended several weeks later, in a fierce battle with an estimated 40,000 Tlascalan warriors under the leadership of Xicotenga. The Tlascalans weren't afraid to move in close to the Spaniards' horses, slashing at the animals' necks and legs with knives made of obsidian (black volcanic glass, similar to granite in hardness). Cortés lost three horses, among them a mare that had recently given birth. The Tlascalans cut her into pieces, sent the pieces to the surrounding villages, then offered her iron shoes to their gods as a tribute.

Cortés's men bitterly resented the danger he'd led them into. How could a few hundred men hold out against tens of thousands of Indians? Word of their complaints got back to Cortés, who called them together. He was a master of the "pep talk," and he reminded them that there was no way to return either to Vera Cruz or to Cuba. He rekindled dreams of treasure in their minds, and by the force of his conviction was able to quiet their anger.

In a broad valley, several days later, Cortés faced another Tlascalan army estimated at 100,000 men. The Indians had painted their bodies bright red with *bixa*—a dye made from the seeds of the annatto tree— giving each screaming warrior the appearance of a devil. However, the Tlascalans advanced in closely packed hordes, which meant that each volley from Spanish cannons killed four to six men at once.

The Indians weren't accustomed to night fighting, but on a moonlit night Cortés's men attacked again. The rush of horses, the roar of cannons, and the fearsome glitter of moonlight on metal armor drove away the Tlascalans, and an uneasy peace was agreed upon. Cortés and his men were exhausted, and spent twenty days resting in Tlascala, the Indians' capital.

As Cortés and his men recuperated, messengers from Montezuma arrived unexpectedly. The Aztec emperor had concluded that neither gifts nor force would be enough to drive the Spaniards away. Therefore, he promised to pay the invaders a yearly tribute—gold, silver, jade, cotton, slaves, anything they desired!—if they agreed to leave his country.

Cortés stubbornly insisted on a personal meeting. Instead, he was invited to the town of Cholula, two days' travel from Tlascala. His new allies urged him not to go, but with his soldiers well-rested, the horses healed from their battle wounds, he was eager to move on.

Cortés and his men were welcomed into Cholula, but once settled they were surrounded and denied food. A woman took pity on Marina, and warned her that the Indians planned to massacre everyone. The evening before the assault, the Cholulans appealed to their gods for victory by sacrificing ten children, five girls and five boys.

The next morning, many Indians gathered in the courtyard, indicating they would be happy to escort the Spaniards safely out of the city. Cortés pretended that he suspected nothing, and invited thirty native priests to his quarters to say farewell. After they arrived, he ordered his men to bar the exits from the compound. A few priests resisted, and were killed outright.

Still pretending to be oblivious of the Cholulans' plot, Cortés mounted his horse. Instead of leaving peacefully, he signaled his artillerymen to begin firing. When the slaughter was over, an estimated six to ten thousand Cholulans lay dead. Cortés dragged the captured priests out to view the body-filled streets, and blamed *them* for the deaths. The priests in turn accused the Aztecs, who, they said, had instigated the plot.

Two weeks later, the invitation finally arrived that Cortés had been waiting for. Montezuma had sent word that the Spaniards would be allowed to enter Tenochtitlán.

FIVE

Meeting Montezuma

On November 8, 1519, after a journey that had lasted two and a half months, covered 250 miles (402 kilometers), and taken them through windswept mountain passes, the Spaniards entered the Valley of Mexico. The sight took their breath away.

Lake Texcoco, reflecting the blue sky above, was as smooth as glass. The whitewashed stone buildings of the island city were decorated with paintings in red, yellow, and black, the sacred colors of the Aztecs. The terraced fields along the shore were well tended, as were the *calmil*, or commoners' household gardens.

The stone causeway from the village of Iztapalapan that crossed Lake Texcoco from the south was five miles (eight meters) long and wide enough for eight horsemen to ride abreast. Indians paddled by in canoes made from hollowed-out logs. *Chinampas*, or floating flower gardens grown on mats woven on reeds and mud, perfumed the air. It

Tlatelolco was the name of Tenochtitlán's richest marketplace. Thousands of Aztecs came there to exchange food, pottery, leather, jewelry, and raw materials imported from as far away as Guatemala. If necessary, Tlatelolco could be defended by warriors stationed offshore in dugout canoes.

was "an enchanted vision. . . . our soldiers asked whether it was not all a dream," wrote Bernal Diaz.

Such beauty didn't fool Cortés, however. He ordered his infantry to march with firearms cocked and crossbows ready.

After a two-mile (three-kilometer) journey along the causeway, Cortés and his men were met by a procession of several hundred Aztec noblemen. Four men carried Montezuma in a golden chair. When the procession halted, the emperor—a slender man whose coal-black hair was cut in straight bangs across his forehead—descended onto a cotton carpet spread by his attendants.

A canopy decorated with green feathers, pearls and gold-and-silver embroidery was held above Montezuma to protect him from the sun. His garments were richly embroidered, and the soles of his san-

THE HIGHLANDS OF CORTÉS'S TIME

The Valley of Mexico, 7,470 feet (2,277 meters) above sea level, is completely surrounded by mountains, which means the heavy rainfall has no way to escape. In 1519, nearly 442 square miles (1,145 square kilometers) of the plateau was covered with water. Over time, the Aztecs enlarged one of the islands in Lake Texcoco by heaping up soft mud from the lake bottom. As the roots of willows and other water-loving plants became interlaced, the mud became more compact, and it was on this island that the Aztecs built their capital, Tenochtitlán. The city was home to about six hundred thousand citizens. Travel to other island villages was by canoe or on foot along the stone causeways. The causeways were interrupted at intervals by wooden bridges that could be drawn up to keep enemies from entering the city or, once they had entered, prevent them from leaving.

dals were made of gold. Montezuma wore a sad expression, perhaps because he'd done his best to avoid such a meeting. Bernal Diaz estimated the Aztec ruler to be about forty years of age. Modern historians believe that Montezuma was actually past fifty.

Montezuma welcomed Cortés to the Aztec capital partly because he believed he had no other choice. The Spaniards were impressed by the luxury they discovered in Tenochtitlán: spectacular gardens, beautiful buildings, and cages filled with exotic birds and animals.

Cortés dismounted, and stepped forward to give the emperor an *abrazo*, a hearty Spanish bear hug. Montezuma's attendants intervened, for it was a breach of manners to treat the emperor so familiarly. However, Cortés was allowed to remove a necklace of pearls and cut-glass beads from around his own neck and place it around Montezuma's.

The Spaniards were escorted to a sumptuous palace that had once been the home of Montezuma's father, Axayacatl. (It was so huge that the six thousand Tlascalan warriors who accompanied Cortés to Tenochtitlán could be housed there too.) Cortés's first precaution was to check the defensibility of the palace. Then he stationed sentries at every entry point.

Montezuma presented Cortés with more gifts, the Spaniards' horses were given hay, and then the visitors were treated to a feast. After the meal, "three tubes much painted and gilded which held . . . herbs which they called *tabaca*" were placed on a table, said Bernal Diaz. Montezuma "inhaled the smoke from one of those tubes."

Montezuma himself lived nearby with his family and about five hundred noblemen and attendants. His palace contained aviaries filled with colorful birds, aquariums full of fish, hanging flower gardens, and a zoo (whose jaguars were said to be fed human flesh). Sunken pools for daily bathing astonished the Spaniards, who rarely bathed, as did the selection of foods on which the Azetc emperor dined. Hundreds of exotic dishes were prepared for him daily, and he picked whichever ones struck his fancy.

The day after his arrival, Cortés took great pains to explain the Christian faith to Montezuma. In turn, the Aztec emperor pointed out that Aztec gods suited the Aztec way of life. He suggested that it would please him if the subject were not mentioned again.

For the next two days, Cortés and his captains explored the causeways, canals, buildings, and markets of Tenochtitlán. They marveled at the cleanliness of the streets and the stone aqueducts that brought fresh water from Chapultepec, the "hill of grasshoppers," on the western edge of the lake. The variety of items for sale at the markets was amazing—all kinds of food, furs, flowers, clothing, gold and silver jewelry, cosmetics, paper, and tobacco. Of course, the Spaniards were repelled by displays of human flesh, also for sale.

On the fourth day, Montezuma granted Cortés's request to climb the 114 stone steps to the top of a temple dedicated to Huitzilopochtili.

Tenochtitlán, a beautiful island ringed by high mountains and surrounded by the blue waters of Lake Texcoco, was the capital of the Aztec empire. Its beauty seemed like an "enchanted vision," said Bernal Díaz.

From its heights, Cortés observed what concerned him most—exactly how the city of 60,000 buildings was laid out. He made a mental note of everything he could see.

Then Cortés and his captains were allowed to enter the inner sanctum of the temple. What they witnessed made them retch. On two altars stood gods encircled by snakes of gold and precious stones. Copal (incense) burned in braziers (metal receptacles filled with live coals), which held several human hearts. The area was "splashed and encrusted with blood . . . in the slaughter houses of Spain there is not such another stench," Diaz wrote.

THE DARK SIDE OF PARADISE

It has been estimated that human sacrifice in Mexico began as early as 5,000 B.C., when the first agricultural settlements were established. The Mayans practiced human sacrifices, as did Indian tribes in the Brazilian jungles, though the numbers of victims were small. The Aztecs adopted the ritual about two hundred years before Cortés's arrival in the New World, and as their empire grew, so did the need for more sacrifices to placate the gods. As a result, one of the Aztecs' aims in making war on their neighbors was not simply to extend their empire, but also to seize prisoners for their bloody altars.

As emperor of the Aztecs, one of Montezuma's most sacred duties was to personally take part in such sacrifices. On the afternoons that he did, he donned the plain white robe of a priest, and mounted the altar steps. A victim was held down on a stone slab, a *tecpatl*, or sacrificial knife made of flint, was plunged into the victim's chest, and the still-beating heart was plucked out and raised aloft as a tribute to the gods. Afterward, Montezuma returned to his palace, bathed in perfumed water, and dressed again in his royal garments. The heart that beat in his chest was at peace, for he believed he had fulfilled his obligations as an Aztec ruler.

Spanish soldiers, like Cortés himself, were merciless on the battlefield, yet were repelled by the Aztec practice of cutting the beating hearts from the chests of sacrificial victims. The practice left Aztec altars black with blood, and filled the air with the stench of death.

In spite of being advised not to mention the matter again, Cortés forcefully informed Montezuma, "these idols of yours are not gods, but evil things that are called devils . . . do me the favour to approve of my placing a cross here on top of this tower."

Montezuma, with equal force, replied that because of the *tatacul*, or sin, that Cortés had committed (of criticizing the gods), it would be necessary for him to perform additional sacrifices. Cortés realized it was useless to argue. "I ask your pardon," he muttered, but his spirit was further hardened against the Aztec practices.

As a peacekeeping gesture, Montezuma allowed the Spaniards to build an altar to their own god in the palace where they were staying. As they did, Cortés's men drew his attention to a portion of a wall that had been freshly plastered. They broke through it, and gasped at what they found—a secret room filled with great quantities of gold, silver, and precious gems that had belonged to Axayacatl. Cortés ordered the wall sealed up, and said nothing to his hosts about the discovery.

Cortés's Tlascalan friends soon warned him that although the Aztecs appeared to be hospitable, they were in fact plotting against their guests. The drawbridges around the city were to be raised to prevent the newcomers from escaping, then they'd all be killed. *Return to Vera Cruz at once!* the Tlascalans advised.

Greed made Cortés hesitate. How could the Aztec treasure be hauled away, or the rest of it located, if they left Tenochtitlán in haste? Besides, wouldn't the long journey to the coast be almost as dangerous as remaining in Tenochtitlán? His captains suggested an alternative to fleeing the city. They pointed out that it would be better "to seize Montezuma than to wait until he attacked us."

Cortés turned the idea over in his mind. ". . . but what possibility is there of our doing a deed of such great daring as to seize such a great prince in his own palace . . . ?" he asked.

Four of his captains—impetuous Alvarado among them—supplied

the answer. "With smooth speeches," they said. The emperor wouldn't be suspicious if Cortés called on him, because the two leaders often visited each other to play cards or *totoloque*, an Aztec game of pitch-and-toss. Once inside Montezuma's palace, he could be seized so swiftly that he'd have no chance to cry out.

The following morning, two Tlascalan messengers arrived from Vera Cruz. They brought news that the Aztecs had killed Juan de Escalante, Cortés's trusted friend, whom he'd left in command of the fort, along with six soldiers and several Indians. It was "the first disaster we had suffered in New Spain," Bernal Diaz remembered. Cortés realized the Aztecs couldn't be trusted. He had no choice but to seize Montezuma, sooner rather than later, and hold him hostage.

SIX

Slaves to Greed

Cortés and his captains paid a call on Montezuma the following day. Cortés chatted amiably, as he often did, then, without warning, accused Montezuma of ordering the attack on Vera Cruz.

The emperor declared that he was innocent of such treachery. Nevertheless, Cortés announced that because of the deaths of Escalante and the six other Spaniards, Montezuma must be placed under arrest. The emperor wept—yet he allowed himself to be taken hostage without calling for help from the three thousand guards who stood nearby.

In Europe, the practice of kidnapping kings or great lords for political advantage was common. It was unheard-of in the Aztec empire, however, where capture usually ended in ritual sacrifice.

To soften Montezuma's humiliation, Cortés assured the emperor that he would be treated as an honored guest, not like a prisoner. He would be allowed to administer his empire until one of Montezuma's warriors,

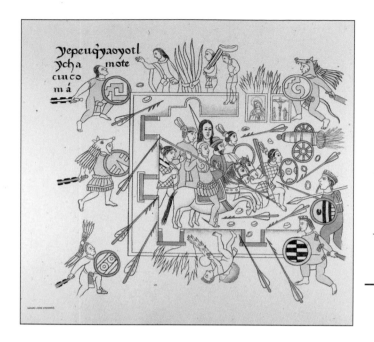

On June 24, 1520, Cortés invaded Montezuma's palace for the second time. When Aztec warriors fought back, Cortés blocked the exits to the courtyard and brutally slaughtered two hundred of them.

Qualpopoca—who'd led the attack on Vera Cruz—returned to Tenochtitlán and could be questioned. Rooms in Axayacatl's palace were converted for Montezuma's comfort. His servants waited on him as before, bringing him specially prepared foods and caring for his personal needs.

Cortés reminded Montezuma, however, that he expected to be compensated in gold. Where, he asked, did the precious yellow metal come from? It was mined at three separate locations, the emperor replied, and offered to have his nobles lead the Spaniards to the sites.

Although Cortés had few men to spare, he selected groups of three or four men to be escorted into the jungle to each of the three Aztec mines. When the men returned, they reported that much more gold could be gotten from each site if better mining practices were used. Later, the Indians told the priest Bernardino de Sahagun how the Spaniards behaved when they saw the mines. They "grinned like little beasts . . . [and] pounded each other with delight. . . . They were slaves to greed."

Three weeks after Montezuma's arrest, Qualpopoca returned to Tenochtitlán. He admitted that he'd killed the Spaniards at Vera Cruz.

He didn't implicate the emperor in any way, which supported Montezuma's claim of innocence.

Qualpococa was tried according to Spanish law, found guilty, and condemned to burn at the stake. (According to one report, he, his sons, and the others tried with him were killed by a barrage of arrows before their bodies were thrown onto a fire.) The Aztecs, although they were accustomed to the bloody sacrifices made to their own gods, had never witnessed executions such as the ones they Spaniards carried out. They were terrified by the sight of their nobles meeting such a fate.

Montezuma wasn't the only one who needed to worry about being taken prisoner, however. In Cuba, Diego Velasquez's rage at Cortés after his flight from Santiago continued to burn. In March 1520, he sent Panfilo do Narvaez to New Spain in command of 18 ships, 1,400 men, 80 horses, and 20 cannons. His orders were to arrest Cortés, even to "cut off his ears."

Cortés understood better than anyone the seductive power of gold, and decided to bribe Narvaez's men to switch their allegiance and come over to his side. In May 1520 , with 260 men and several thousand Tlascalan warriors, Cortés headed for the coast. He left Alvarado in charge of a small force in the capital. As long as Montezuma was held hostage, he believed, the Spaniards would be safe in Tenochtitlán.

A heavy rainstorm blew in about three miles from the village of Cempoala, where Narvaez had set up his headquarters. It was unusual to attack during bad weather, but Cortés struck at midnight in a drenching downpour. Taken by surprise, Narvaez's men stumbled over each other in the wet, inky darkness, then surrendered after a short battle, during which Narvaez suffered the loss of an eye.

By daylight, Cortés renewed friendships with his defeated countrymen, many of whom he'd known well in Cuba. He promised to give them a share of the Aztec wealth if they pledged their loyalty to him. They were as tempted by greed as he was himself, and eagerly switched sides.

Cortés left the Aztec capital in March 1520, accompanied by a few hundred Indian allies. He hurried back to Vera Cruz, where Panfilo de Narvaez had come ashore, ordered by the governor of Cuba to arrest Cortés as a traitor. The explorer defeated Narvaez in a nighttime battle, and bribed his men to come over to his side.

Before Cortés could savor his victory, however, messengers brought news of an uprising in Tenochtitlán. The Aztecs had attacked Alvarado, who was barricaded inside Axayacatl's palace. Montezuma was still a prisoner, but might soon be freed. Without taking time to rest, Cortés made a forced march back to Tenochtitlán to lift the siege.

On June 24, 1520, he entered the capital and found it eerily silent. Cortés's army, reinforced with Narvaez's men, numbered more than one thousand soldiers and one hundred cavalrymen. The Aztecs weren't prepared—yet—to confront a force three times larger than the one that had left the city a month earlier.

Cortés demanded an explanation from Alvarado, who said he'd learned that a ceremony called Toxcatl would be held in the square in front of Axayacatl's palace. He'd believed it was actually a prelude to an attack on his small force, so instead of delaying action, he'd followed Cortés's example of striking first. He'd blocked the exits from the square, and then the Spaniards had drawn their swords and slaughtered two hundred Aztecs. Enraged by the massacre, other Indians had forced the Spaniards back into their quarters.

Cortés, who'd had no difficulty entering the palace, now realized he'd allowed himself to be trapped. Although Spanish artillery took its toll in the battle that followed, the Indians advanced in great human waves. The Spaniards built three barricades-on-wheels (wooden walls mounted on rollers), behind which they tried to force their way out of the courtyard. The Indians attacked so fiercely that they were driven back inside the palace again.

Finally, Cortés turned to the only man who could quiet the murderous mob outside. He demanded that Montezuma speak to his people so that further bloodshed could be avoided on both sides.

Montezuma went to the rooftop of the palace and called out to those below. But his people had come to despise their emperor for allowing himself to be taken prisoner. They jeered, and hurled a barrage of stones at him. One of them struck Montezuma on the head. He collapsed, and died on June 30, 1520. Having been scorned by his subjects, it was said, he preferred death to life.

Inside the palace, the Spaniards' supplies of food, water, and gunpowder ran short. After repeated efforts to reach a truce with the Aztecs failed, Cortés decided to make a break for freedom along the causeway that linked Tenochtitlán to the city of Tacuba, on the western edge of Lake Texcoco.

Since the Aztecs had removed their bridges, the Spaniards built a portable one. Before leaving the palace, Cortés divided the treasure from

Portraits of
Montezuma
and Cortés

Axayacatl's secret room among his men, many of whom weighted themselves down with as much as they could carry. It proved to be a fatal mistake.

Early in the predawn darkness of July 1, 1520, only eight months after entering Tenochtitlán, the Spaniards sneaked along the causeway. They placed the portable bridge across the first gap, crossed it safely, then proceeded to the next one. An old woman spotted them and gave an alarm. Thousands of Aztecs spilled out of their hiding places and seized many Spaniards in the rear columns. Alvarado narrowly escaped, and Cortés was wounded. Other Spaniards, weighed down with gold, drowned in the black waters along the causeway when the portable bridge collapsed. Four hundred fifty Spanish soldiers, over four thousand Indian allies, and forty-six horses perished. Ever after, the Spanish called it the *Noche Triste*, the Sad Night.

Since Montezuma had no male heir, Cuitlahuac (some historians identify him as Montezuma's brother, others as his nephew), was placed on the Aztec throne. Montezuma had been a voice of prudence, but with his death the Indians refused to consider overtures for peace. In the beginning, they'd believed the Spaniards were invincible gods. Now, they realized that they bled and died like ordinary mortals. They also knew they had the advantage of numbers over Cortés. It was inevitable that the final confrontation between the two cultures would be the bloodiest of all.

SEVEN
The Siege of Tenochtitlán

As the Sad Night paled to dawn, Cortés and his men staggered into the village of Tacuba. About 450 soldiers survived the flight. There were only twenty-four horses left. Cortés's knee was so badly damaged he was afraid to dismount for fear he'd be unable to get back on his horse. A day later, as the Spaniards made their way south to Tlascala, Cortés's skull was fractured by a rock hurled by the pursuing Aztecs.

In the Otumba Valley, the Otomi Indians, who'd been recruited by the Aztecs, waited in ambush for the battle-weary invaders. The Spaniards' cannons lay at the bottom of the lake and few of their crossbows were in working order. They had only swords, daggers, and lances, so combat was one-on-one. Weakened though he was, Cortés ran the Otomi chief through with a lance, causing the other Otomis to flee in panic.

At Tlascala, Cortés collapsed and lay unconscious for several days, during which time two fingers on his battered left hand were ampu-

Cortés was enraged by the treachery of the Tepeacan Indians, who pledged their allegiance to him, then switched it back to the Aztecs. In retaliation, he branded men, women and children.

tated. Throughout the ordeal, Marina remained faithful and nursed him. After twenty days, Cortés's wounds had healed enough that he was able to ride again. One of his first decisions was to attack the Tepeacans, whose province was about fifty miles (eighty kilometers) from Tlascala.

The Tepeacans had pledged their allegiance to him, then switched it back to the Aztecs. Their treachery infuriated Cortés. He gathered his men together, plus seventeen horses that were well enough to be ridden, and, accompanied by 40,000 Tlascalan warriors he descended on Tepeaca. The invasion was successful, and the defeated Indians awaited their fate, convinced that only their deaths would satisfy Cortés. However, he knew that being taken into slavery was a great humiliation to the Indian spirit. So he branded his former allies as slaves—men, women, and children—with the letter *g*, for *guerra*, the Spanish word for war.

Other tribes feared similar retaliation, so the Spaniards were unmolested as they proceeded south, toward the coast. Yet there was another reason the journey to the coast was uneventful. An invisible but deadly ally had come to Cortés's aid. One of Narvaez's men had been infected with smallpox, and the virus was spreading through the highlands like wildfire. The Aztecs, who had never been exposed to the virus and had built up no immunity to it, died by the thousands. One of the first victims was the new emperor, Cuitlahuac. At his death, another of Montezuma's relatives, eighteen-year-old Cuauhtemoc, became the last Aztec ruler of Mexico.

When Cortés arrived at Vera Cruz, he was pleased to find a ship in the harbor. A few days later, a second arrived. Velasquez, unaware that Narvaez's mission had failed, had sent additional men and supplies. As before, Cortés craftily offered gold to the newest arrivals in exchange for their allegiance. He had severely punished the Tepeacans for switching sides, but saw nothing contradictory about encouraging fellow Spaniards to do the same.

Reinforced by new men and fresh arms, Cortés turned his attention to what had been on his mind from the moment he was driven from Tenochtitlán. He would return to the highlands and subdue the Aztecs permanently. A different kind of man—this one was bruised, missing two fingers, and had a fractured skull—might have given up. Not Cortés.

But the Aztecs—even as they suffered and died from smallpox—were equally determined that the Spaniards would be slaughtered if they tried to enter the Valley of Mexico again. Occupants of villages along the way to Tenochtitlán were ordered to dig trenches in which pointed stakes were driven to disable men and horses. Ambush sites were built on every hillside. Spies kept track of all movement throughout the valley.

In order to carry out such defenses, the Aztec had to threaten the smaller tribes. The result wasn't what they had in mind. Although the Indians pretended to be submissive to their Aztec masters, they saw a chance to be free of their domination, and secretly allied themselves with the Spaniards.

Six months after his exodus from Tenochtitlán, Cortés took stock of his situation. The weather was cool. The rainy season was over. Men and horses were well rested. He had several cannons and other artillery, plus 20,000 Tlascalan warriors at his command. It was worrisome that gunpowder was in short supply, but on December 28, 1520, Cortés and his army began the 250-mile journey back to Tenochtitlán, picking up warriors from other tribes as they marched along.

When he arrived in the Valley of Mexico, Cortés set up camp in the village of Texcoco, on the eastern edge of the lake. His men—especially the new recruits—complained that it would impossible to recapture the city with such a small force. Once again, there was talk of mutiny. Cortés executed one of the malcontents, Antonia de Villafana, squelching further rumors about turning back.

The shortage of gunpowder still concerned Cortés. But his spirits were lifted when messengers reported that another ship had arrived at Vera Cruz with a large supply. He ordered that the gunpowder be brought to the highlands immediately. Also newly arrived at Vera Cruz was a Spanish shipbuilder, Martin Lopez, a *hidalgo* like Cortés himself, who had little hope of becoming rich unless he came to New Spain and took the same risks Cortés had.

In the autumn of 1520, Cortés set Lopez to building thirteen brigantines, which were finished by the end of February 1521. The vessels were tested on a dammed-up river near Tlascala, then dismantled and carried 50 miles (80 kilometers) overland by 8,000 Indian porters. The ships were reassembled at the edge of Lake Texcoco, then put into the water on April 28, via a 12-foot-(3.6-meter) wide, 0.5-mile-(0.8-kilometer) long canal that Indian workers had spent seven weeks diggings. Sentries were posted each night as the brigantines were rebuilt, because after dark the Aztecs sneaked across the lake by canoe and tried to burn them.

Cortés sent word to Tenochtitlán that he wanted most of all to restore harmony between Spaniards and Aztecs. The offer was rebuffed. Cortés was disappointed, because he was genuinely reluctant to mount an all-out attack on the city, which he'd once admired for its beauty, order, and cleanliness.

In April 1521, Cortés assessed his military strength. He had about 900 Spaniards, which included 86 horsemen, 118 men armed with crossbows, and the remainder with lances, pikes, shields, and daggers. He also had at least 75,000 Indian volunteers. It was time to make a final assault on the city that had been the center of Aztec life for two centuries.

One of Cortés's first acts was to deprive the capital of drinking water by destroying the freshwater aqueducts. The brigantines were launched down the canal, Cortés himself commanding *La Capitana*. As the armada moved under a light wind toward Tenochtitlán, it was approached by five thousand large canoes, each manned by up to twenty of the fiercest Aztec warriors.

The wind picked up, filling the sails of the brigantines, enabling them to ram the smaller Aztec craft and dump their occupants into the water. Crossbows and cannon were fired into the floundering mob, turning Lake Texcoco red with blood. Those who did not die by gunfire drowned. Although the Indians lived on an island in a lake, most of them didn't know how to swim.

The battle, which moved from water to land and back again, lasted a week. Cortés was reinforced by increasing numbers of Indian warriors from other villages—Chalcans, Xochimilcans, Otomis, and members of other smaller tribes—who saw more clearly than ever a chance

Cortés ordered the construction of thirteen brigantines—small sailing vessels—and used them for a final assault on Tenochtitlán in April 1521.

---

to defeat the dreaded Aztecs. Cortés tightened the noose around Tenochtitlán with each passing day. Even so, he continued to urge the Aztecs to surrender. They refused. He decided there was only one solution—to completely destroy their fabled city.

The Aztecs had concentrated their forces in the marketplace, which the Spaniards had once marveled at. Cortés's first assault ended badly, with more than sixty Spaniards killed or captured and the loss of seven or eight horses. Cortés himself was wounded again. On an evening in June 1521, the Spaniards were grief-stricken to have to watch from afar as their companions who'd been captured were sacrificed by the Aztecs. The soldiers' beating hearts were cut from their bodies, their corpses dismembered and thrown down the steps of the temple. Any lingering remorse Cortés had about destroying Tenochtitlán vanished that night.

The siege of Tenochtitlán lasted seventy-five days. An estimated 240,000 Aztecs were killed, and thousands more died of starvation and disease. Among Cortés's Indian allies, 30,000 thousand perished before the city fell on August 13, 1521. According to the Catholic calendar, it was the day of Saint Hippolytus, a Christian martyr. A church dedicated to him was later built in the former kingdom of the People of the Sun. In the end, Cortés not only defeated the Aztecs, but had the satisfaction of imposing Christian saints on them as well.

In the aftermath of the siege, Cortés's Indian allies looted the homes of their former conquerors. The stench of thousands of rotting corpses filled the air. In an ancient poem, the proud and powerful Aztecs had mused,

> *Oh princes,*
> *Who could conquer Tenochtitlán?*
> *Who could shake the foundations of heaven?*

They couldn't have known the answer would be a man called Cortés.

E I G H T

Everything Became Thorns

Tenochtitlán, which Bernal Diaz called "an enchanted vision," lay in ruins. Cortés and his men withdrew to the village of Coyoacan while the Aztecs collected their dead. The bodies were burned in huge fires in the streets and marketplaces of the once-great city.

When young Cuauhtemoc was captured, Cortés promised the boy he'd be safe in Spanish hands. But when Cuauhtemoc refused to reveal the hiding place of the remaining Aztec wealth, Cortés allowed the young man to be tortured. The truth was that much of the treasure had been lost in the waters of Lake Texcoco during the Spaniards' flight on the Sad Night. The riches Cortés's men gleaned from their adventure were meager indeed. A cavalryman's share turned out to be one hundred gold pesos, or one-fifth the price of a horse!

To ease the discontent among his men, Cortés awarded them *encomiendas*, or grants of land and slaves. Not surprisingly, he gave

Cortés accepted the surrender of eighteen-year-old Cuauhtemoc, the last ruler of the Aztec empire, promising to protect him from harm. Later, believing that Cuauhatemoc had conspired against him, Cortés ordered his execution.

himself the largest grant of all. But for such transactions to be legal, Cortés needed the approval of King Charles, which he didn't have. The *encomienda* system was further complicated by the arrival of Spanish settlers from Cuba, who'd heard of the fall of Tenochtitlán and come to stake claims of their own.

In the summer of 1523, word came from Madrid that solved the problem. King Charles had appointed him the captain-general of New Spain.

Armed with the king's blessing, Cortés quelled any attempts to overthrow his authority. He also rebuilt Tenochtitlán and renamed it Mexico City, as suited its role as the capital of a new Mexico. Aztec temples and palaces were demolished, then buildings of European design were erected in their place. The first Catholic church in Mexico was built on the ruins of Huitzilopochtli's temple. Cortés asked King Charles to send priests to New Spain to help Christianize the Indians. In 1522, two Franciscan monks arrived, followed in 1524 by twelve more.

ROMANCE WAS NEVER SIMPLE

Early in 1522, Cortés's loyal companion, Marina, presented him with a son, whom he named Martin, in honor of his father. In August 1522, no doubt to Cortés's surprise, his legal wife, Catalina, and her brother Juan arrived from Cuba. The reunion in Tenochtitlán between husband and wife was short, for Catalina died suddenly. Juan accused Cortés of murder, but the charges were never proved.

But Cortés hadn't satisfied his lust for gold or glory. In 1523, he dispatched an expedition to Guatemala under the command of his friend Alvarado to search for treasure. A larger force led by Cristobal Olid, the former quartermaster at Vera Cruz, was sent to Honduras the same year.

In 1524, Cortés supervised the construction of a *zócalo*, or new town square, in Mexico City and laid the foundation for the future home of the Hospital of Jesus, which is still in operation today. He built a palace for himself, whose stone walls were thick enough to withstand a cannon's blast. He hired butlers, guards, and servants of all kinds. To quell Indian resentment, he insisted that Cuauhtemoc accompany him everywhere to demonstrate that all was well in the new kingdom.

In 1524, tin was discovered in Taxco. When it was mixed with copper, Cortés was able to make bronze and manufacture his own field

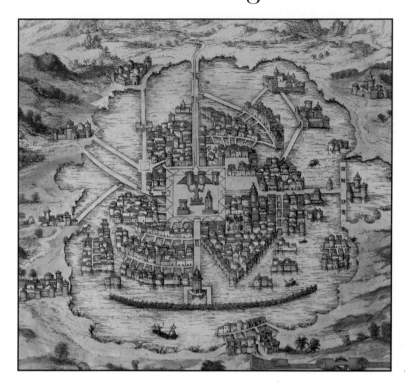

An imagined aerial view of Tenochtitlán, renamed Mexico City after Cortés defeated the Aztecs, shows the stone causeway that linked the island to the mainland.

artillery. Iron, too was found, so cannons could be made, as well. Such discoveries meant he no longer needed to depend on Spain to supply him with weapons.

Cortés still had many enemies, among them a priest, Bartolomé de Las Casas, who reported to King Charles that Cortés was despoiling Mexico. Others whispered that Cortés wasn't satisfied with being a captain-general but yearned to be the king of New Spain. Nor did mutiny cease to be a problem for Cortés. In Honduras, Olid betrayed him, switching his allegiance to Velasquez.

Cortés set out to arrest his former comrade, taking Cuauhtemoc and two Aztec priests with him to ensure safe passage through hostile territory. As always, Marina accompanied him. (Aguilar had died, and she was now his primary translator.)

In a violent showdown with Olid, Cortés ordered the beheading and dismemberment of his longtime acquaintance, as a warning to any

Cortés built a palace in Cuernavaca, one of Mexico's most beautiful cities, for his young Spanish bride, Juana de Zuniga. During the reign of the Aztecs, the hills west of Cuernavaca were devoted to warrior cults.

Spaniard who might be considering mutiny. Cortés—who had criticized the cruel sacrifices of the Aztecs—was capable of behaving mercilessly toward his own countrymen when it was required.

The return trip to Tenochtitlán lasted a year and a half, because Cortés made the fateful mistake of trying to cross the Yucatán Peninsula through the province of Tabasco. As the Spaniards traveled through the dense rain forest, where natives traveled not on foot but mostly by canoe, they became hopelessly lost.

The water in the marshes was undrinkable. Supplies ran low. Men and horses died. When Cortés learned that Cuauhtemoc and the two priests, seeing the weakened condition of their captors, were plotting to assassinate him, he responded as was now his custom. They were executed immediately. Bernal Diaz confessed to having grown fond of the young emperor, and regretted Cortés's action.

On April 25, 1526, having finally reached the coast of Honduras, Cortés set out for Mexico, but his ship was blown off course and ended up in Cuba. He'd left Santiago in 1519, seven years earlier, and he was welcomed back like a hero. Velásquez had died, so there was little need to fear imprisonment. Cortés rested in Cuba for ten days, then sailed again for Mexico to restore order to Tenochtitlán.

Meanwhile, one-eyed Narvaez had denounced Cortés before the Council of the Indies. A royal commission, including Juan Ponce de Leon (related to the explorer who'd searched for the Fountain of Youth), was sent to Mexico to investigate the financial arrangements, debts, and appointments that Cortés had made since becoming captain-general.

Cortés welcomed the commissioners with a grand feast, but soon after, many became ill. Days later, Ponce de Leon and thirty others, including two priests, were dead. Cortés was never accused of murder, but suspicions that he'd poisoned them ran high.

By the autumn of 1528, Cortés realized the only way to save his good name and his property was to return to Spain and speak to King Charles on his own behalf. He assembled an entourage, as befitted the conqueror of Mexico.

To impress the king, he collected as much gold, silver, and jewels as could be found. Among Cortés's personal possessions were five perfect emeralds that Montezuma had given him, for which he soon found a special use. Wild animals unknown to Europeans—armadillos, jaguars, and opossums—were taken aboard, as were many Indian dancers, jugglers, and acrobats.

King Charles gave Cortés a royal welcome, made him a marquis, and promised him one-twelfth of any future wealth that might be discovered in Mexico. In addition, he granted Cortés an *encomienda* in Mexico encompassing 25,000 thousand square miles and an additional 23,000 thousand slaves. Fine rewards, yet Cortés's dream of glory fell short of what he'd imagined. He'd hoped to be made a duke.

King Charles also blessed Cortés's marriage to Juana de Zuniga, the duke of Bejar's niece. Juana was young and pretty, and brought Cortés a handsome dowry, in addition to important connections at court. As a wedding gift, Cortés presented her with Montezuma's five perfect emeralds.

In 1530, Cortés left Seville with his new wife, arriving in Vera Cruz on July 15. He built his bride a palace in Cuernavaca, one of the most beautiful cities in Mexico, and they had a child. He established a sugar mill, and planted wheat, grape vines, and olive trees. He introduced African slaves to Mexico, and imported pigs, cattle, sheep, horses, and donkeys from Europe.

His activities stop there. He hoped to find a shortcut to China. In 1533, he sent a naval expedition north that landed at the tip of Baja California. It's possible that he gave the area its name (after Queen Califia, the fictional character of a popular novel). All the while, he continued to live beyond his means and fell into debt.

Old deeds returned to haunt him as the past was dug up by his enemies. What really happened to the Aztec treasure on the Sad Night? How did Catalina die? What about the deaths of the commissioners? Official investigations were conducted, as they are in modern times, and Cortés's reputation became more tarnished than before.

In 1540, he returned to Spain to reclaim his fame and replenish his fortunes. This time, his reception at court was quite different from what it had been ten years earlier. King Charles was in Flanders, and his representatives turned a cold shoulder to Cortés's pleas.

The achievements of the man who'd conquered the vast Aztec empire by exercising extraordinary boldness now seemed irrelevant.

THE FATE OF CORTÉS'S FAVORITES

Father Olmedo died in 1524. Cortés had his old friend Cristobal Olid executed in 1524. Gonzalo de Sandoval, whom Cortés had fondly called *hijo*, died in 1528 in Palos, Spain. Pedro de Alvarado became the first governor of Guatemala, and was killed in 1541 in a fall from his horse. Marina, the mother of Cortés's oldest son, married Juan Jaramillo, the captain of one of the brigantines. Bernal Diaz wrote *The Reminiscences of Bernal Diaz del Castillo*, an account of Cortés's expedition, and died in 1584.

Cortés said that never again was he "lucky in anything . . .everything became thorns." His health failed. Bowing to age—he was fifty-five years old—and to his changed circumstances, he spent the remainder of his life at Castilleja de la Cuesta, a castle near Seville. In the end, the public recognition that he'd craved as much as wealth eluded him.

When he felt death approaching, Cortés made plans to return to the land of his greatest victories. A final bout of illness prevented him from leaving Spain, and he died in Castilleja de la Cuesta on December 2, 1547, at age sixty-three.

In death, Cortés was as restless as in life. He was buried first near Seville, then reburied in Texcoco in 1566, almost twenty years later. In September 1821, when Mexico declared its independence from Spain, the new government ordered the destruction of Cortés's remains. A Spanish historian, Lucas Alaman, stole the casket away to a secret hiding place.

One hundred years later, during the Mexican Revolution of 1920, the casket was moved again to keep it safe from the nationalists, who hated any reminder of the Spanish conquest. In 1946, following clues left in old documents, archeologists discovered the casket and its bones hidden deep within a wall at the Hospital of Jesus.

Today, the casket is enclosed in a cement wall near the altar of a small church adjoining the hospital, marked by a plaque that draws little attention from passersby. A portrait of Cortés hangs in a boardroom at the hospital, one of the few painted during his lifetime. Yet in all of modern Mexico no statues of the Spanish *conquistador* can be found. After almost five hundred years, he is still despised as the man who, with a few hundred soldiers, ruthlessly destroyed an entire culture in the name of glory, gold, and God.

Afterword

The question is often asked, how could Hernando Cortés, so recently arrived in a foreign land with only a few hundred soldiers, have conquered an empire defended by hundreds of thousands of warriors?

Part of the answer must lie in the shrewd decisions that Cortés made. One of his first steps was to recruit allies from the smaller tribes that made up the Aztecs' kingdom. He played on their antagonism toward their conquerors and used it for his own purposes.

Cortés was also able to take advantage of Montezuma's indecisiveness. The Aztec emperor's hesitancy—in the face of the Spaniards' boldness—made him a victim rather than a victor. Then, at the end, Cortés was aided by a deadly ally—smallpox—which devastated the Indian masses, who had no immunity to the disease. Due to the epidemic that swept the highlands, the population of the Valley of Mexico, estimated in the millions in 1519, was reduced to nine hundred thousand by 1521.

Afterword

Was Cortés a wicked and evil man, as he is so often portrayed? It cannot be denied that he massacred many Indians, and enslaved and tortured others. He seized property, leaving the Indians landless, and he encouraged the imposition of the Catholic faith on a people who had a religion of their own.

Cortés was, in fact, a reflection of his counterparts in other European nations. England, France, Holland, Italy, and Portugal all sought to colonize the New World, and practiced the same indignities on native peoples as did Cortés. Such men had few scruples when it came to achieving their ends.

One assessment can be made about Cortés with which no one will argue. He was true to the Spanish proverb, "Fortune always favors the bold." Long before the Puritans arrived in the New World, Cortés had already changed forever the future of the Americas.

Cortés and His Times

1485   Hernando Cortés is born in Medellín, Spain, in the province of Estremadura.

1499-1501   Cortés attends the University of Salamanca.

1504   Cortés joins Nicolas de Ovando in Santo Domingo.

1511   Cortés accompanies Diego Velasquez to Cuba.

1518   Cortés is named *caudillo* (leader) of the expedition to the Yucatán.

1519   Cortés builds a settlement called "Rich City of the True Cross" (Vera Cruz); Cortés arrives at Tenochtitlán; he meets Montezuma; nine days later, Montezuma is kidnapped.

1520   Montezuma is stoned to death. The Spaniards escape from Tenochtitlán and that night is called *Noche Triste*, the Sad Night.

1521   The Aztecs surrender.

1524   The Hospital of Jesus is built in center of Tenochtitlán, which now called Mexico City.

1526   Cortés returns to Cuba for the first time in 7 years.

1528   Cortés returns to Spain, after an absence of 25 years.

1530   Cortés marries Juana de Zuniga; he returns to Mexico.

1533   Cortés sends a naval expedition north that discovers Baja California.

1540   Cortés returns to Spain to reclaim hia fame.

1547   Cortés dies in Seville at the age of 63.

BIBLIOGRAPHY

Carrasco, David. *City of Sacrifice: The Aztec Empire and the Role of Violence in Civilization.* Boston: Beacon Press, 1999.

Carrasco, David, and Eduardo Matos Moctezuma. *Moctezuma's Mexico: Visions of the Aztec World.* Niwot, CO: University Press of Colorado, 1992.

Diaz del Castillo, Bernal. *The Discovery and Conquest of Mexico, 1517-1521.* Leonard, Irving A., editor. New York: Farrar, Straus & Cudahy, 1956.

Foster, Lynn V. *A Brief History of Mexico.* New York: Facts on File, 1997.

Madariaga, Salvador de. *Hernan Cortés: Conqueror of Mexico.* New York: Macmillan Company, 1941.

Marks, Richard Lee. *Cortés: The Great Adventurer and the Fate of Aztec Mexico.* New York: Alfred A. Knopf, 1993.

Meyer, Michael C., and William L. Sherman. *The Course of Mexican History.* New York: Oxford University Press, 1979.

Miller, Robert Ryal. *Mexico: A History.* Norman, OK: University of Oklahoma Press, 1985.

Newcom, Covelle. *Cortez, the Conqueror.* New York: Random House, 1947.

Robinson, Henry Morton. *Stout Cortez: A Biography of the Spanish Conquest.* New York: The Century Co., 1931.

Smith, Michael E. *The Aztecs.* Oxford, U.K.: Blackwell, 1996.

Thomas, Hugh. *Conquest: Montezuma, Cortés, and the Fall of Old Mexico.* New York: Simon & Schuster, 1993.

Thompson, J. Eric Sidney. *Mexico Before Cortez: An Account of the Daily Life, Religion and Ritual of the Aztecs and Kindred Peoples.* New York: Charles Scribner's Sons, 1933.

FURTHER RESEARCH

Websites:

Hispanos Famosos

http://coloquio.com/famosos/cortes.html

Hernando Cortes

http://www2.worldbook.com/features/features.asp?feature=cinco&page=html/cortes.htm&direct=yes

Books:

Crisfield, Debbie. *The Travels of Hernan Cortés*. Austin: Steadwell Books, 2000.

Helly, Mathilde, and Rémi Courgeon. *Montezuma and the Aztecs*. New York: Henry Holt, 1996.

Jacobs, William Jay. *Cortés: Conqueror of Mexico*. New York: Franklin Watts, 1994.

Lilley, Stephen R. *Hernando Cortés*. San Diego, CA: Lucent Books, 1996.

Stein, R. Conrad. *Hernando Cortés*. Chicago: Childrens Press, 1991.

Source Notes

Foreword

p. 4: "the people of the dogs": Robert Ryal Miller, *Mexico: A History* (University of Oklahoma Press, 1985), p. 42.

Chapter 1:

p. 8: "famous races of men": Salvador De Madariaga, *Hernan Cortes: Conqueror of Mexico* (Macmillan Company, 1941), p. 19.

p. 8: "so ill that he was often on the verge of death": Henry Morton Robinson, *Stout Cortes: A Biography of the Spanish Conquest* (The Century Company, 1931), p. 7.

p. 10: "a rushing river": Robinson, p. 8.

p. 11: "made much noise in the house of his parents": de Madariaga, p. 25.

p. 11: "as good a face to losses as to gains": de Madariaga, p. 22.

p. 13: " Neither in this Island nor in any other": Robinson, p. 14.

Chapter 2:

p. 14: "dine to the sound of trumpets": Hugh Thomas, *Conquest: Montezuma, Cortes, and the Fall of Old Mexico* (Simon & Schuster, 1993), p. 132.

p. 17: "a disease that could only be cured by gold": Shannon Garst, *Three Conquistadores: Cortes, Coronado, Pizzaro* (Julian Messner, 1947), p. 22.

p. 17: "They stuffed themselves with it…[and] were slaves to greed": Conrad R. Stein, *Hernando Cortes* (Children's Press, 1991), p. 67.

p. 18: "I knew him to be …full of courage": Robinson, p. 29.

p. 18: "above all things": Garst, p. 15.

p. 21: "roared with rage": Stephen R. Lilley, *Hernando Cortes* (Lucent Books, 1996), p. 25.

p. 21: "Years from now": Robinson, p. 47.

Chapter 3:

p. 20: "Gentlemen, are you Christians?" Thomas, p. 163.

p. 23: "These Indians…believe that [horses] go to war": Mathilde Helly, Remí Courgeon, *Montezuma and the Aztecs* (Henry Holt, 1996), p. 37.

p. 24: "ten bronze cannon": Thomas, p. 172.

Chapter 4:

p. 32: "heart [was] anguished": Thomas, p. 179.

p. 32: "sorcerers attempted to shame him": David Cararsco, Eduardo Matos Moctezuma, *Moctezuma's Mexico: Visions of the Aztec World* (Univeristy Press of Colorado, 1992), p. 145.

Source Notes

p. 35: "Fortune always favors the bold": Richard Lee Marks, *Cortes: The Great Adventurer and the Fate of Aztec Mexico* (Alfred A. Knopf, 1993), p. 189.

Chapter 5:

p. 42: "an enchanted vision": Michael E. Smith, *The Aztecs* (Blackwell, 1996), p. 1.
p. 45: "three tubes much painted and gilded": Robinson, p. 220.
p. 46: "splashed and encrusted with blood": Robinson, p. 155.
p. 48: "these idols of yours are not gods": Diaz, p. 220.
p. 48: "I ask your pardon": Diaz, p. 220.
p. 48: "to seize Montezuma": Diaz, p. 227.
p. 48: "the first disaster we had suffered": Diaz, p. 228.

Chapter 6:

p. 52: "cut off his ears": Thomas, p. 369.

Chapter 7:

p. 63: "Oh princes, who could conquer Tenochtitlan": Davis Carrasco, *City of Sacrifice: The Aztec Empire and the Role of Violence in Civilization* (Beacon Press, 1999), p. 33.

Chapter 8:

p. 71: "everything became thorns": de Madriaga, p. 460.

Afterword:

p. 74: "Fortune always favors the bold": Marks, p. 189.

Index

Page numbers in **boldface** are illustrations.

maps
  New World (1563), 15
  to Tenochtitlán, 29, 37

army, 21, 33, 35, 38, 52–53,
    57, 59, 60, 61, 64–65, 71
Aztecs, 4–5, **5, 17,** 23,
    26–32, **31,** 38, 40, 41,
    42, **42,** 43–56, 59, 60,
    61–64, 73

battles, 16, 25–26, **27,** 38, 39,
    54, 61–63, **62**
bridges, 43, 48, 54–56, **67**

California, 70, 75
captives, 16, 22, 24–25, 40,
    50–51, 62–63
Charles I (King), 34, **34,** 35,
    65, 69, 70
Cholulans, 39–40
Columbus, Christopher, 5–7,
    6, 13
Cortés, Hernando, **9, 55**
  as captain-general, 65–69,
    68
  children, 28, 66, 70
  death, 71–72
  education, 10–11
  finances, 10, 11, 18, 19, 20,
    70
  as marquis, 69
  as mayor, 16, 35
  personality, 35–36, 38
  plantation, 13–16
  romances, 11, 16, 28, 66,
    70, 75
  in Spain, 69–71, 75
  success factors, 73–74
  as traitor, 35, 52, **53,** 59, 69

wounds, 55, 57–58, 62
youth, 7, 8–10, 11, 75
Cuauhtemoc, 64, **65,** 66,
    68–69
Cuba, 7, 14–16, 69
Cuitlahuac, 56, 59

dates, 75
Diaz, Bernal, 21, 42, 43
disease, 59, 73
dogs, 27–29

gold, 17, **17,** 18, 21, 26–27,
    29, 42–43, 45, 48, 51,
    52, 54–56, 64, 69
Guatemala, 66

Hispaniola, 12, 13, 14
Holy Roman Empire, 34
Honduras, 66, 67
horses, 20, 26, 38
human sacrifice, 23–24, **24,**
    31–32, 32–33, 38, 45,
    46–48, **47,** 62–63

Lake Texcoco, 41, 43, 64
land, 13–16, 64, 65, 70, 74
Las Casas, Bartolomé de, 67

Marina (Malinche), 26, 28,
    28, 39, 58, 67, 71
Mexico City, 65, 75
Montezuma, 27, 30, 39,
    42–43, **44,** 45, 47, 49,
    50, 54, **55,** 73, 75
murders, 66, 69, 70, 71
mutiny, 35, 60, 67–68

Narvaez, Panfilo do, 52, **53,**
    69

Native Americans, 16–18, 20,
    22, **23,** 25, 56, 57,
    59–60, 61–63, 73, 74.
    See also Aztecs;
    Cholulans; slavery;
    Tlascalans; Totonacs

Quetzalcoatl, 30, **31,** 32, **32**

religion, 17, 18, **19,** 22–24,
    24, 30, **30,** 32, **32,**
    45–48, 63, 65

Sad Night, 56, 75
slavery, 12, **12,** 14, 26, 28,
    58–59, 60–61, 64, 70

Tabascans, 25, **27**
Tenochtitlán, 26–30, 40, **42,**
    43–49, **46,** 53–56, 65,
    67
  journeys to, **29, 37,** 41,
    60, 69
  siege of, 61–63
Tepeacans, **58,** 58–59
Tlascalans, 38, 39, 48, 57–58
Totonacs, 32–33
translators, 24–25, 26, 28,
    28, 67

Valley of Mexico, 41
Velazquez, Diego, 14, 16, 18,
    20, 21, 52, 59, 67
Vera Cruz, 33–35, 38, 49, 50,
    75

weapons, 25–26, 30, 39, 59,
    60, 67

Yucatan, 16–21, 23, 25–27, 75